LET'S FIND
WHEELS
AND AXLES

by Wiley Blevins

raintree
a Capstone company • publishers for children

A WHEEL SPINS. An AXLE SPINS TOO.

An axle is a bar or rod that goes through the wheel. Did you know a wheel and axle is a simple machine? With a wheel and axle, you can move things from here to there.

Where can you find wheels and axles? Let's have a look! They are all around us!

PIZZA TIME!

Roll the pizza cutter back and forth. It has a small wheel and axle.

5

HOP ON A BIKE.

It has two wheels and axles. They spin round and round.

READY TO GET WHERE YOU'RE GOING FAST?

6

WHAT IS A UNICYCLE?

It's a bike with one wheel and axle. The performer rides by. Where will she go?

WHEREVER SHE GOES, IT WILL BE FUN!

LOAD ON THE BOXES!

This trolley has two wheels and an axle. It moves big, heavy boxes easily.

STACK UP THE BOXES ONE BY ONE.

WHEELS AND AXLES

help this boy move from here to there.

BIG WHEELS TURN AS THE BOY ROLLS ALONG.

SEE THE TOYS?

Give them a push. Their wheels and axles spin and turn.

THEY ZIP AWAY FAST.

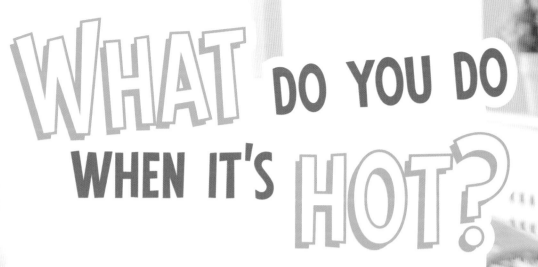

WHAT DO YOU DO WHEN IT'S HOT?

Find a fan. Its blades are a wheel spinning on an axle.

AHHH! FEEL THE COOL AIR.

KNOCK, KNOCK!

Even a door needs a wheel and axle. Twist the doorknob. It is a wheel turning the axle.

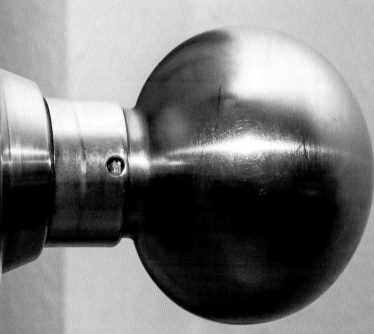

WHERE'S THE HANDLE FOR THIS DOOR?

It doesn't need one!
Why? This door is a wheel
that spins. Step in.
But don't spin too fast.

YOU MIGHT END UP OUTSIDE AGAIN!

DID YOU KNOW A TOILET PAPER ROLL IS A WHEEL?

It spins on a little rod. That's its axle. Spin the roll. Get as much as you need.

BUT DON'T FORGET TO FLUSH.

OH, NO!

You can't write with a broken pencil tip. What will you do? Find the pencil sharpener. Use the handle. It's an axle.

SPIN, SPIN, SPIN.

NOW YOUR PENCIL IS SHARP AGAIN.

SPIN THE ROUNDABOUT!

Use your hands and feet to push this big wheel. Then hop on and hold on tight.

UP, UP, UP.

Go round and round. The Ferris wheel is in town. It spins on an axle.

WHAT CAN YOU SPY FROM THE TOP OF THIS FUN RIDE?

pizza cutter

roundabout

toilet paper holder

trolley

doorknob

bike

pencil sharpener

revolving door

toy truck

unicycle

wheelchair

fan

Ferris wheel

Raintree is an imprint of Capstone Global Library Limited, a company incorporated in England and Wales having its registered office at 264 Banbury Road, Oxford, OX2 7DY – Registered company number: 6695582

www.raintree.co.uk
myorders@raintree.co.uk
Copyright © Capstone Global Library Limited 2022

ISBN 978 1 3982 0507 9 (hardback)
ISBN 978 1 3982 0508 6 (paperback)

Edited by Erika Shores
Designed by Kyle Grenz
Media Researcher: Tracy Cummins
Production by Spencer Rosio
Originated by Capstone Global Library Ltd
Printed and bound in India

Image Credits
Getty Images: ONOKY - Fabrice LEROUGE, 20–21; Shutterstock: 9comeback, 30 middle left, Ake-Aud Pitugbood, 2–3, AnnGaysorn, 12–13, Beautiful landscape, 31 bottom right, denisik11, 31 top left, fizkes, 14–15, JANNTA, 30 bottom right, Kuznetsov Alexey, 8–9, LightField Studios, 10–11, Ljupco Smokovski, 31 middle right, Mike Flippo, 30 middle right, Monkey Business Images, 6–7, MriMan, 31 top right, MrVander, Design Element, Neamov, 30 top left, New Africa, 22–23, Oleg Mikhaylov, 26–27, PERLA BERANT WILDER, 30 bottom left, Polhansen, 28–29, PR ImageFactory, 16–17, rungrote sommart, 30 middle, s_oleg, Cover, shutterdandan, 4–5, siraphat, 31 middle left, Titikul_B, 18–19, US 2015, 24–25, vilax, 30 top right, wanphen chawarung, 31 bottom left

British Library Cataloguing in Publication Data
A full catalogue record for this book is available from the British Library.

FIND OUT MORE ABOUT SIMPLE MACHINES BY CHECKING OUT THE WHOLE SERIES!